MATH WORKBOOK

BRAIN QUEST®

PRE-KINDERGARTEN

workman

• New York •

This book belongs to:

First Name

Last Name

Workman Kids
Workman Publishing
Hachette Book Group, Inc.
1290 Avenue of the Americas
New York, NY 10104
workman.com

Workman Kids is an imprint of Workman Publishing, a division of Hachette Book Group, Inc. The Workman name and logo are registered trademarks of Hachette Book Group, Inc.

Written by Bob Krech and Jeff Grabell
Illustrations by Jennifer Bartlett
Art direction by Keirsten Geise
Produced for Workman Publishing by WonderLab Group, LLC, and Fan Works Design, LLC.

The publisher is not responsible for websites (or their content) that are not owned by the publisher.

Workman books may be purchased in bulk for business, educational, or promotional use. For information, please contact your local bookseller or the Hachette Book Group Special Markets Department at special.markets@hbgusa.com.

ISBN 978-1-5235-2420-4

First Edition July 2024

Distributed in Europe by Hachette Livre, 58 rue Jean Bleuzen, 92 178 Vanves Cedex, France.

Distributed in the United Kingdom by Hachette Book Group, UK, Carmelite House, 50 Victoria Embankment, London EC4Y 0DZ.

Printed in China on responsibly sourced paper.

10 9 8 7 6 5 4 3 2 1

DEAR PARENTS AND CAREGIVERS,

We are excited to partner with you and your child on this quest for knowledge! Written to supplement a full year of math learning, Brain Quest workbooks guide kids through concepts using multiple approaches, clear instruction, and fun illustrated examples.

Pre-Kindergarten children learn foundational math concepts, including:

- Numbers
- Counting
- Comparing
- Shapes
- Sorting
- Patterns

Brain Quest activities are designed to promote critical thinking and creative problem-solving skills, encourage task persistence, and engage kids through fun to instill a love of learning!

Going on this adventure alongside your child will strengthen these skills, so enjoy helping your child learn!

Onward to the quest!

—The editors of Brain Quest

CONTENTS

Hi! I'm Amanda the Panda
and I'm here to guide you on your quest!

Check out the map at the back of this book.
As you work through these pages, I will remind
you to put a sticker on the map to celebrate
your progress. I will also pop in with tips to
help you on your way.

Are you ready to learn and have some fun?
Let's go!

zero

Trace the **0** with your finger.
This puppy has **0** spots.

Circle the puppy with **0** spots.

Trace the number **0** with a pencil.
Start at the **red** dot.

Write the number 0.
Start at the **red** dot.

Circle the dish with **0** bones.

Great job! You know that zero means none!

Hidden Zeroes

Color each space with a **0** yellow.

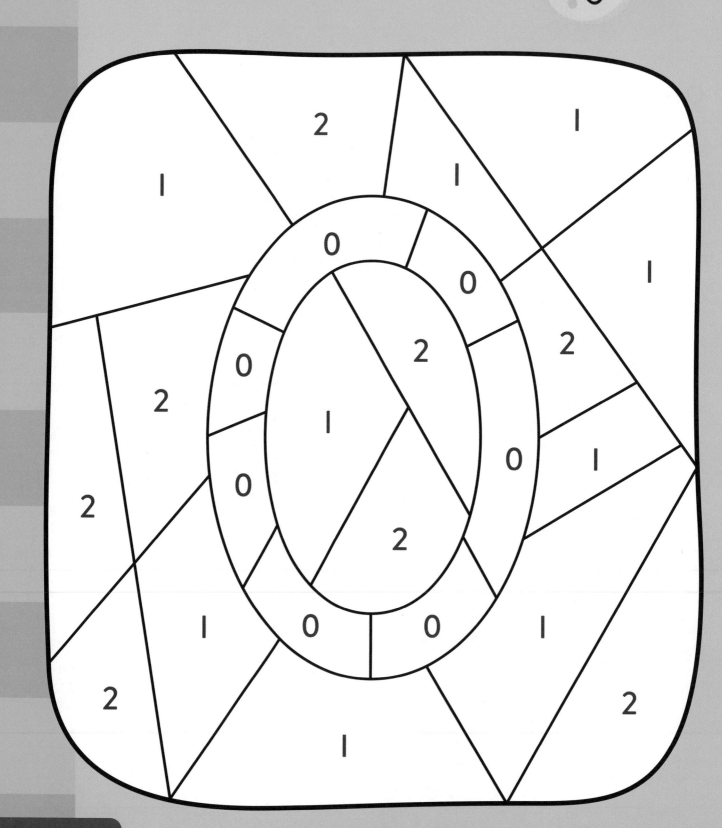

Brain Quest Math Workbook: Pre-Kindergarten

one

Trace the **I** with your finger.
Count the orange.

Color **I** orange.

Trace the number **I** with a pencil.
Start at the **red** dot.

Numbers 0 to 5

Write the number 1.
Start at the red dot.

• • • • • •

Circle each monkey with 1 banana.

Apple Trees

Color the apple trees with **l** apple.

Draw **l** apple on the tree.

Numbers 0 to 5

2
two

Trace the **2** with your finger.
Count the bongos.

Draw **2** horns on the bongo's head.

Trace the number **2** with a pencil.
Start at the **red** dot.

2 2 2 2 2 2

Write the number 2.
Start at the **red** dot.

Color the animals that are in groups of 2.

Brain Quest Math Workbook: Pre-Kindergarten

Numbers 0 to 5

Safari

Circle the animals that are in groups of 2.

3
three

Trace the **3** with your finger.
Count the eggs.

Circle each nest with **3** eggs.

Trace the number **3** with a pencil.
Start at the **red** dot.

3 3 3 3 3 3

Write the number 3.
Start at the **red** dot.

Draw and color **3** eggs in the nest.

Bird Watching

Count the birds. Write the number of birds in the box.

Numbers 0 to 5

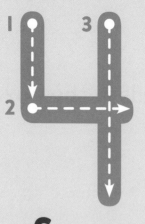

four

Trace the **4** with your finger.
Count the fish.

Color **4** fish.

Trace the number **4** with a pencil.
Start at the **red** dot.

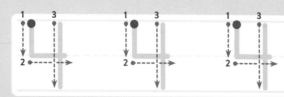

Write the number **4.**
Start at the **red** dot.

Count the sea animals. Color each group of **4.**

Sharks

Count the sharks in each group.
Draw a line to the matching number.

1

2

3

4

Brain Quest Math Workbook: Pre-Kindergarten

5
five

Trace the **5** with your finger.
Count the candles.

Draw **5** candles on the cake.

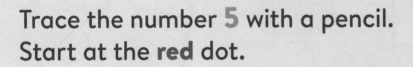

Trace the number **5** with a pencil.
Start at the **red** dot.

5 5 5 5 5 5

Numbers 0 to 5

Write the number 5.
Start at the **red** dot.

Count and color the party hats.

Birthday Presents

Count the presents in each group.
Circle the group with **5** presents.

Numbers 0 to 5

Same Number

Count the apples. Count the oranges.
Draw a line to match groups with the same number.

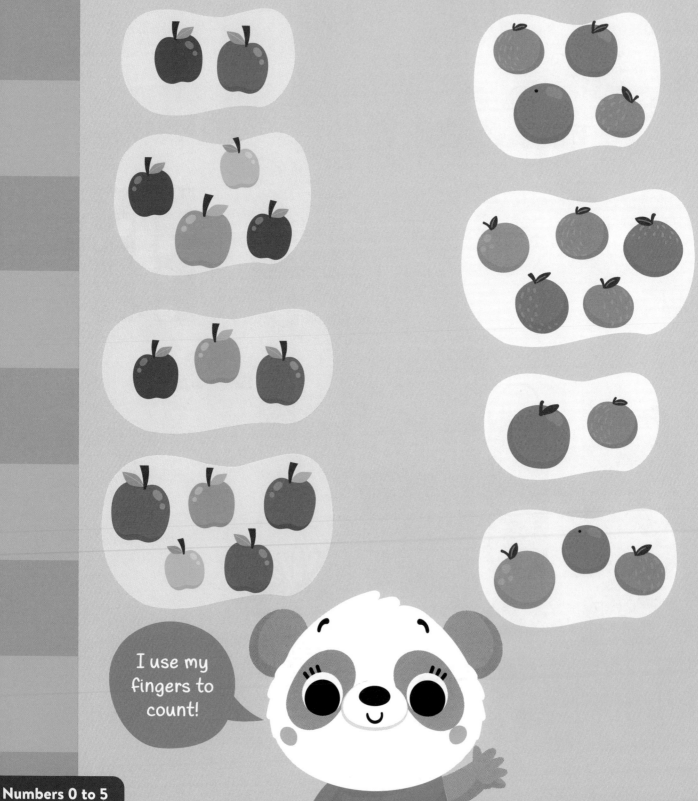

I use my fingers to count!

Brain Quest Math Workbook: Pre-Kindergarten

In the Ocean

Connect the dots from 0 to 5.
Color what is swimming in the water.

0
1
2
3
4
5

Team Time!

Trace the numbers from **0** to **5**.

Block Color!

Look at each number. Color that many blocks!

1

2

4

You know your numbers from 0 to 5! Put a sticker on your map!

Numbers 0 to 5

6
six

Trace the **6** with your finger.
Count the flowers.

Count the petals on each flower.
Circle each flower with **6** petals.

Trace the number **6** with a pencil.
Start at the **red** dot.

6 6 6 6 6 6

Write the number 6.
Start at the red dot.

Count the flowers in each vase.
Write the number of flowers in the box.

Hidden 6s

Find and circle the hidden 6s.
Look for other groups of 6 objects!

7

1

seven

Trace the **7** with your finger.
Count the colors in the rainbow.

Color your own rainbow.

Trace the number **7** with a pencil.
Start at the **red** dot.

7 7 7 7 7 7

rain Quest Math Workbook: Pre-Kindergarten

umbers 6 to 10

Write the number 7.
Start at the red dot.

Draw lines to put the **7** ducklings in the tub.

Brain Quest Math Workbook: Pre-Kindergarten

Cleaning Up

Count the objects in each group.
Draw a line to the matching number.

4

5

6

7

Numbers 6 to 10

eight

Trace the **8** with your finger.
Count the ants.

Color the **8** ants.

Trace the number **8** with a pencil.
Start at the **red dot**.

Write the number 8.
Start at the **red** dot.

• • • • • •

Count the legs on the spider.
Write the number of legs in the box.

Bug-o-Mania

Touch and count the insects.
Circle each group with **8** insects.

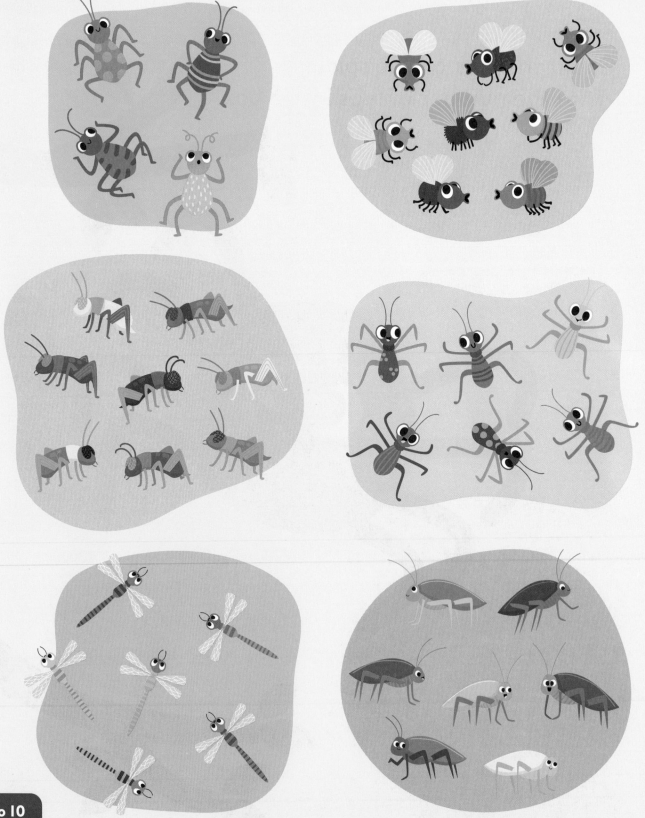

Brain Quest Math Workbook: Pre-Kindergarten

nine

Trace the **9** with your finger.
Count the frogs.

Color **9** lily pads.

Trace the number **9** with a pencil.
Start at the **red** dot.

Numbers 6 to 10

Write the number 9.
Start at the red dot.

• • • • • •

Touch and count the sloths.
Write the number of sloths in the box.

Rain Forest

Circle each jaguar with 9 spots.

Touch and count the toucans.
Write the number of toucans in the box.

Numbers 6 to 10

10

ten

Trace the **10** with your finger.
Count the paintbrushes.

Draw a handle on each of the **10** paintbrushes.

Trace the number **10** with a pencil.
Start at the **red** dots.

Write the number 10.
Start at the red dot.

• • • • • • • • • • •

Color each of the 10 spots a different color.

Brain Quest Math Workbook: Pre-Kindergarten

Numbers 6 to 10

Crayons

Count the crayons in each box.
Draw a line from each box to the matching number.

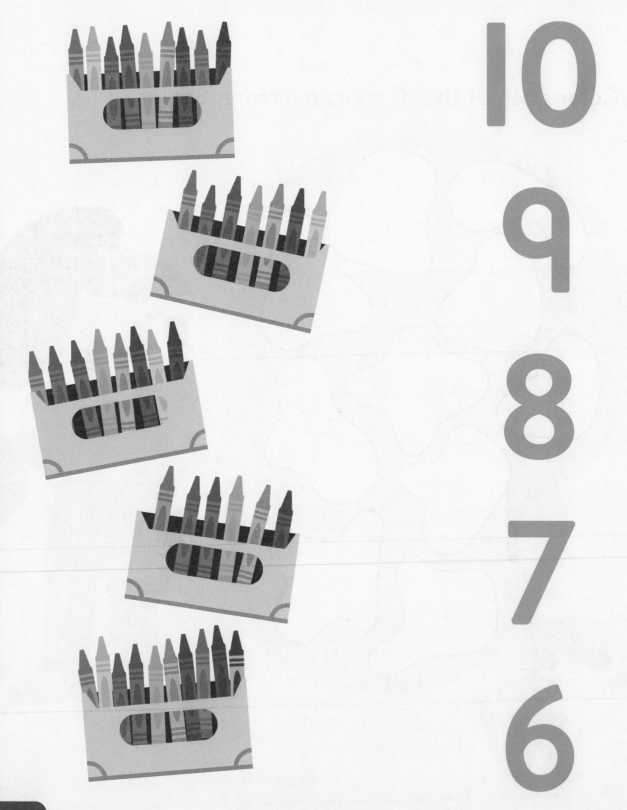

10

9

8

7

6

Beach Fun

Draw a line from each sun to an umbrella.
Count the umbrellas and the suns.
Write the number of each in the boxes.

Count the pails.
Write the number of pails in the box.

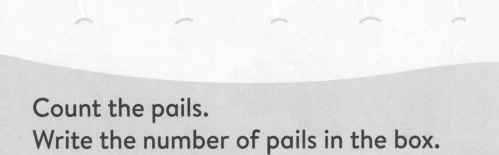

Numbers 6 to 10

In the Park!

Count each squirrel, kid, and dog.
Write the number of each in the box.

Cross things out as you count them!

 squirrels

 kids

 dogs

Brain Quest Math Workbook: Pre-Kindergarten

Hello, Friend!

Connect the dots from **0** to **10**.
Color the friend you see!

Great counting!

Numbers 6 to 10

All Aboard

Write the missing numbers to count from **0** to **10**.

Color by number. See who is going for a ride.

Brain Quest Math Workbook: Pre-Kindergarten

Numbers 6 to 10

Lots of Spots

Draw spots on each ladybug to match the number.

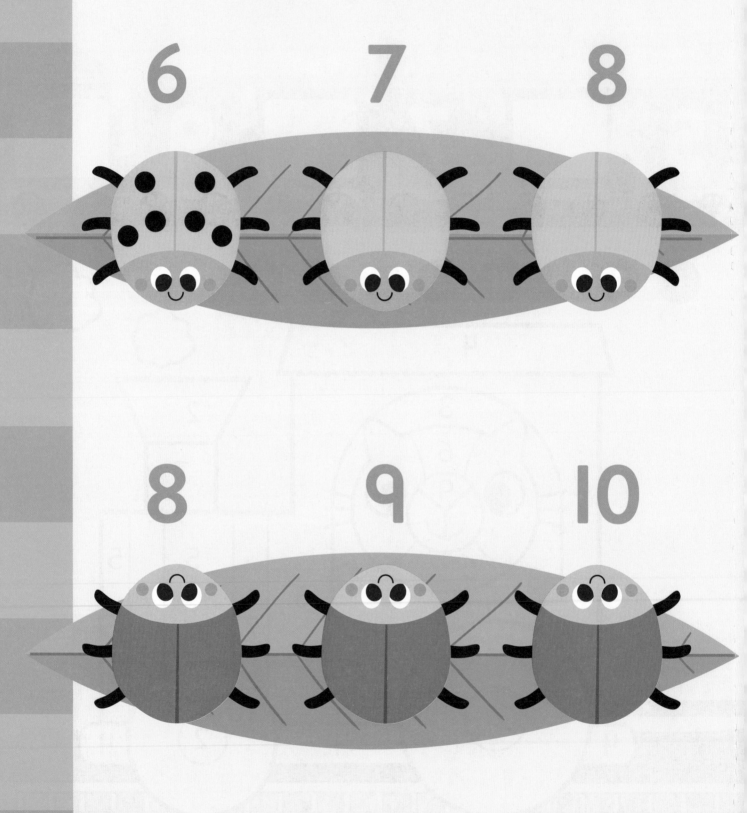

6   7   8

8   9   10

Brain Quest Math Workbook: Pre-Kindergarten

Time for Toys

Count the toys in each group.
Write the number of toys in the box.

0 to 10 is a snap!
Put a sticker on
your map!

dinosaurs	dolls	trucks	balls

Food Fiesta

Count the tacos and the chips.
There are **more** tacos than chips.
There are **fewer** chips than tacos.

3   **2**

more   **fewer**

Count the chips in each group.
These groups are **equal**.

2   **2**

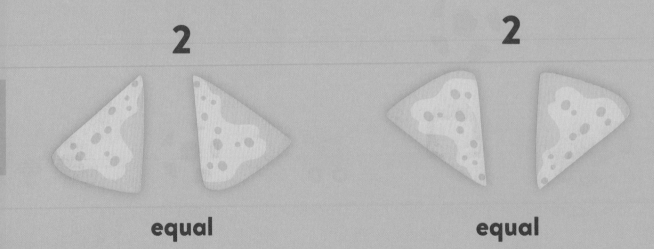

equal   **equal**

Color the group with **more** tacos **green**.

Color the group with **fewer** tacos **red**.

Draw an **equal** number of tacos.

How Sweet!

Circle the kid in each group that has **more**.

Brain Quest Math Workbook: Pre-Kindergarten

Sushi

Look at each tray.
Draw an X on the group that has **fewer** pieces.

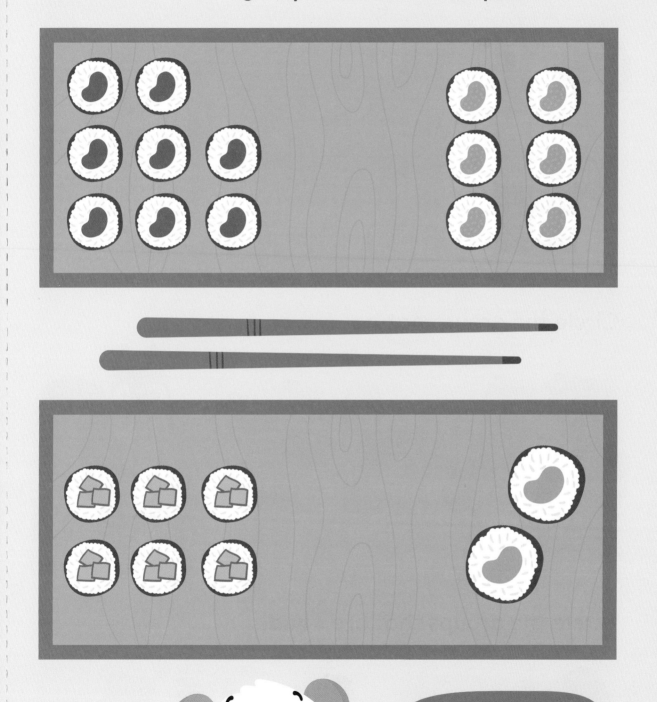

Point to each item as you count. Say the number out loud.

Comparing

Nutty

Count the nuts in each group.
Circle the group that has **more**.

Circle the group that has **fewer**.

Circle the groups that are **equal**.

Brain Quest Math Workbook: Pre-Kindergarten

Bake Off!

Draw a line from each hat to a baker.
Draw a line from each baker to a bowl.

Are there enough hats and bowls for every baker?
Circle **Yes** or **No**.

Yes No   Yes No

Comparing

Set the Table

Guests are coming for dinner.
Draw enough plates for everyone.

How many forks do you count?

Winter Hats

These winter hats are the **same.**

These winter hats are **different.**

Circle the winter hats that are the **same.**
Draw an X on the winter hat that is **different.**

Comparing

Mittens

Circle the mittens in each group that are the **same.**

Walk On!

Circle the pair of shoes in each group that is **different**.

It's a Pair

Draw a line from each shoe to the matching one.

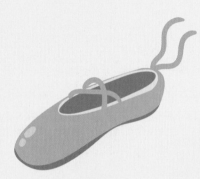

Brain Quest Math Workbook: Pre-Kindergarten

Pajama Party

Color the pajamas so they are the **same**.

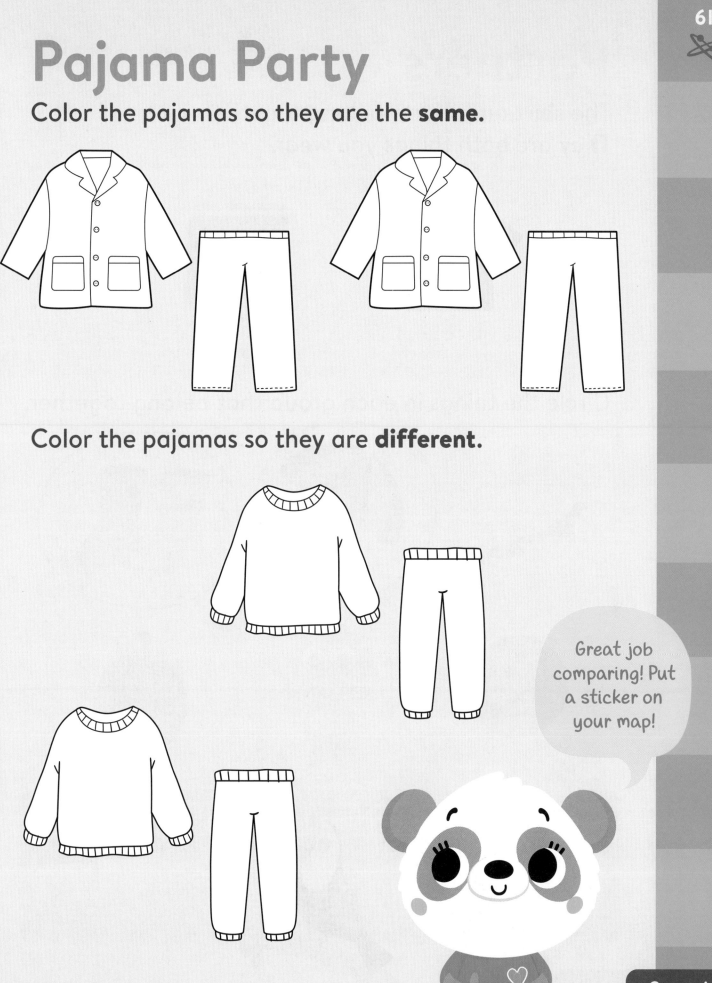

Color the pajamas so they are **different**.

Great job comparing! Put a sticker on your map!

Comparing

Partners

The shirt and shorts belong together.
They are both things you wear.

Circle the things in each group that belong together.

Brain Quest Math Workbook: Pre-Kindergarten

A cow and a pig are both animals. They belong together!

Brain Quest Math Workbook: Pre-Kindergarten

Blocks

Draw lines to sort the blocks by color.

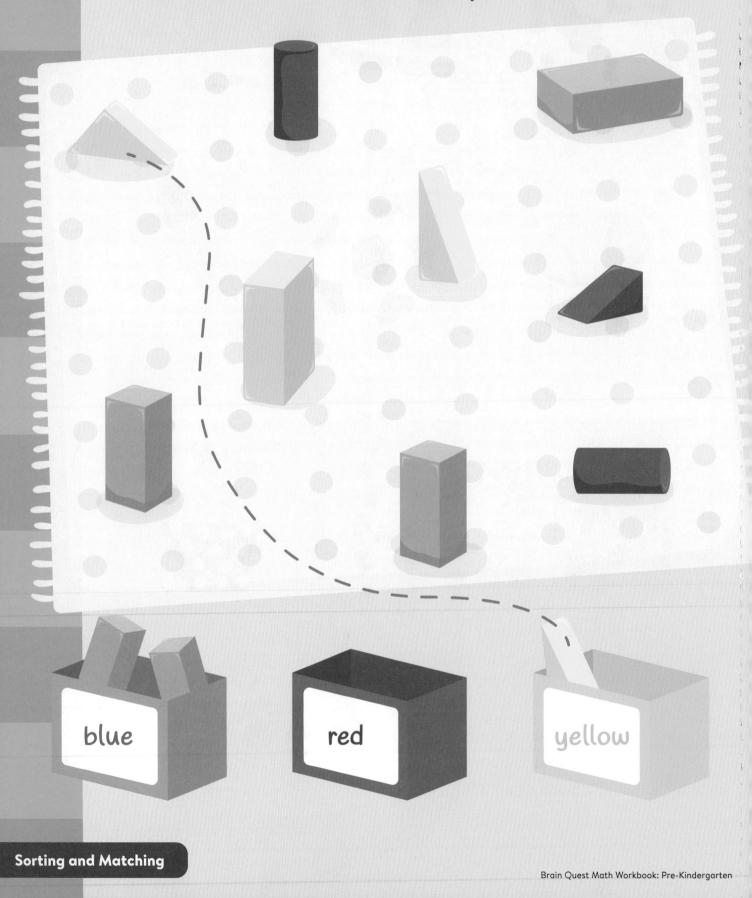

blue

red

yellow

Time to Play

Draw an X on the items that do NOT belong on a playground.

Sorting and Matching

Animal Homes

Draw a line from each animal to its home.

Together!

Draw something that belongs in this group.

Great job! Put a sticker on your map!

Sorting and Matching

Handy Hands

You can use your fingers to count on.

What is **1** more than **2**?

Start at **2**.
Count **1** more.
It's **3**!

Start at **3** and count **1** more.
Write the number in the box.

Fingers are a math tool that is always with you!

Brain Quest Math Workbook: Pre-Kindergarten

Count on to find out how many.
Write the number in the box.

What is 1 more than 4?

2 3 4

1

What is 1 more than 2?

2

1

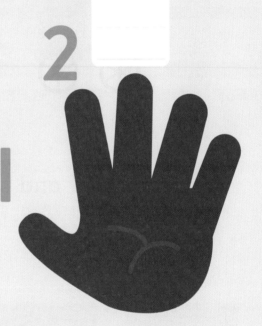

What is 1 more than 1?

1

Choo, Choo!

Count the train cars to find how many in all.
Write the number of train cars in the box.

I and I more is [   ].

2 and I more is [   ].

Brain Quest Math Workbook: Pre-Kindergarten

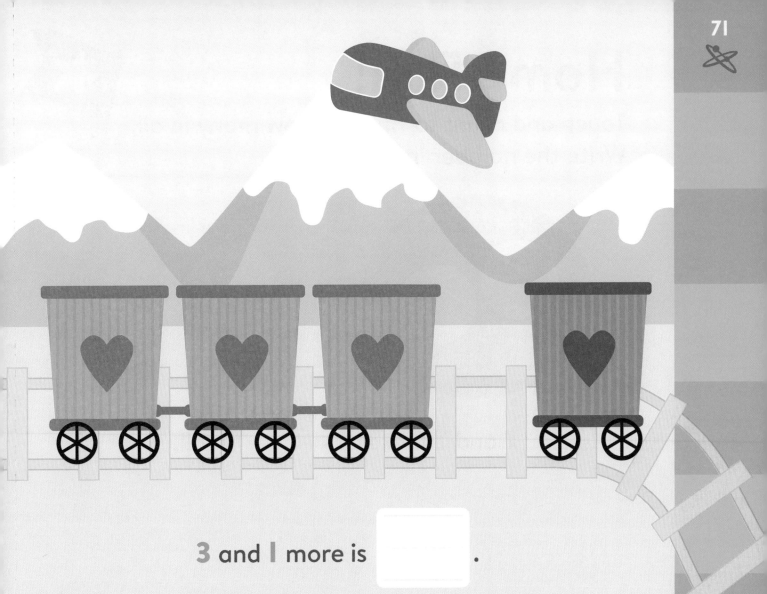

3 and 1 more is [   ].

4 and 1 more is [   ].

Counting through 10

Home Run!

Touch and count to find out how many in all.
Write the number in the box.

2 and **2** more is [ ] in all.

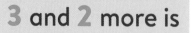

3 and **2** more is [ ] in all.

Brain Quest Math Workbook: Pre-Kindergarten

Fab Food

Touch and count to find out how many in all.
Write the number in the box.

3 and 2 more is ⬜ in all.

4 and 1 more is ⬜ in all.

1 more is 1 bigger!

2 and 1 more is ⬜ in all.

Counting through 10

Dippity Dots!

Count the dots and write the number in the box.

|1| and |2| more is **3** in all.

and more is **4** in all.

Brain Quest Math Workbook: Pre-Kindergarten

and ___ more is **5** in all.

and ___ more is **5** in all.

and ___ more is **4** in all.

Brain Quest Math Workbook: Pre-Kindergarten

Fly Away

You can take away from a number.
Count to find out how many are left.

2 take away 1 is ⬚ .

There is 1 balloon left.

3 take away 1 is ⬚ .

Brain Quest Math Workbook: Pre-Kindergarten

Ships Ahoy!

Count the boats in each group.
Take 1 away.
Count and write how many are left.

5 take away 1 is [ ].

4 take away 1 is [ ].

Monster Trucks

Count the trucks in each group.
Take **2** away.
Count and write how many are left.

4 take away 2 is ☐.

5 take away 2 is ☐.

When you take away, you have less.

Count the trucks in each group.
Take **3** away.
Count and write how many are left.

4 take away 3 is [ ].

6 take away 3 is [ ].

5 take away 3 is [ ].

In the Woods

Count the animals in each group.
Take **4** away.
Count and write how many are left.

5 take away **4** is [   ] .

7 take away **4** is [   ] .

Sky High

Count the birds in each group.
Take **5** away.
Count and write how many are left.

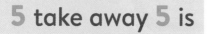

5 take away **5** is [ ] .

When we take away everything, we are left with zero!

10 take away **5** is [ ] .

Blast Off!

Count back to send the rocket into space.
Write the missing number in the box.

10

9

[ ]

7

6

[ ]

4

[ ]

2

[ ]

0

Before and After

What comes before? What comes after?
Write the missing number in the box.

| 1 | 2 | 3 |

| | 4 | |

| | 3 | |

Math Hands

Use your fingers to count back.

What is **1** less than **4**?

Start at **4** and count back to find out. Write the number in the box.

What is **1** less than **3**? Write the number in the box.

Brain Quest Math Workbook: Pre-Kindergarten

Count back to find out how many.
Write the number in the box.

What is **1** less than **5**?

5

What is **1** less than **3**?

3 4
5

What is **1** less than **2**?

2 3 4
5

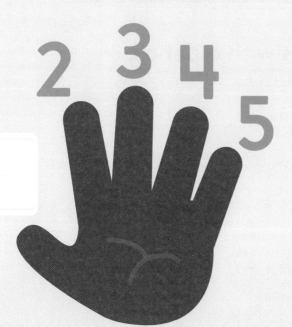

Great job!
Put a sticker
on your map!

Rectangles

A **rectangle** has 4 straight sides.

There are
2 short sides.

There are
2 long sides.

Trace the flag with your finger.

Trace the rectangles with a pencil.

Modern Art

Color each rectangle a different color.

How many rectangles are there in all?
Write the number in the box.

A rectangle can lie
on its long side or
its short side.

Shapes and Patterns

Rectangle Rescue

Count the rectangles in each row.
Write the number of rectangles in the box.

Squares

A **square** is a special type of rectangle.

All **4** sides are straight.

All **4** sides are the same length.

Trace the frames with your finger.

Trace the squares with a pencil.

Shapes and Patterns

4 Corners

Color each large square **orange**.
Color each small square **pink**.

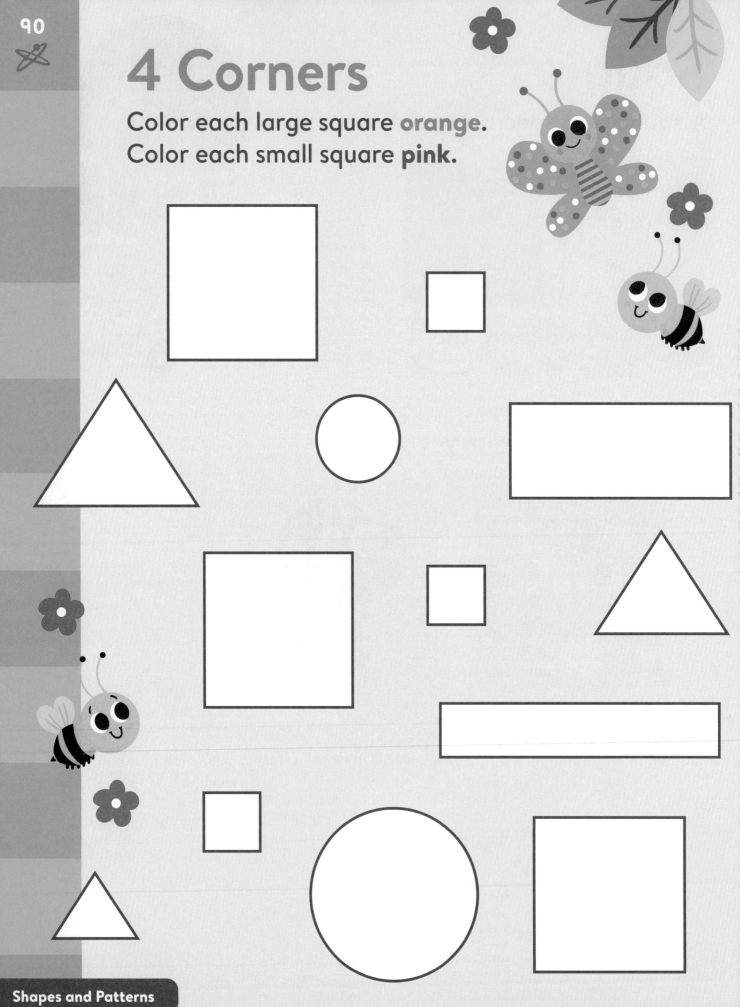

Brain Quest Math Workbook: Pre-Kindergarten

Find That Square

Draw an X on each square in the picture.

Brain Quest Math Workbook: Pre-Kindergarten

Circle Time

A **circle** is a round shape.
It has no sides.
It has no corners.

Trace the circles with your finger.

Trace the circles with a pencil.

Bubbles!

What shape are bubbles? Circles!
Draw lots of bubbles!

Shapes and Patterns

All Around

Color each object that is a circle.

Draw a smiley face.
That's a circle too!

Brain Quest Math Workbook: Pre-Kindergarten

The Missing Hat

Amanda the Panda has lost her favorite hat.
Follow the path of circles to help her find it!

Shapes and Patterns

Triangles

A **triangle** is a shape with **3** straight sides.

It has **3** corners.

Trace the triangles with your finger.

Trace the triangles with a pencil.

Twirling Triangles

These triangles have flipped and turned!
Draw a line to match each triangle with its partner.

You can
flip or turn
a triangle.
It is still a
triangle!

Shapes and Patterns

Triangle Time

Find the triangles
and color them.

Brain Quest Math Workbook: Pre-Kindergarten

Match It Up

Draw a line to match the big and little triangles.

Shapes and Patterns

Picnic!

Count the shapes.
Write the number of each shape in the box.

Trace the shapes as you count them!

▭	◻	◯	△

Treasures!

Draw lines to match each shape to the correct treasure chest.

Colorful Kites

Color the kites to match the shapes.

Draw and color 2 more kites.

Butterfly

Color the spaces in the picture to match the shapes.

Shapes and Patterns

Matchmaker

Find your way with your finger!
Connect each shape to its match.

Brain Quest Math Workbook: Pre-Kindergarten

Making Shapes

Trace the colored shapes with your finger.

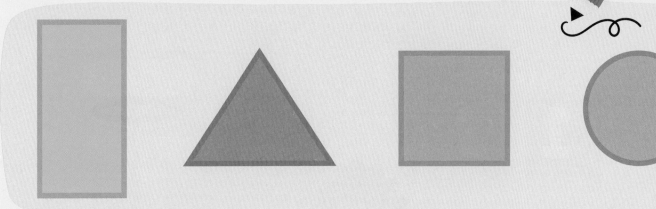

Trace the shapes with a pencil.

Draw your own shapes.

Get in Shape

Count the shapes in the picture.
Write how many there are in the boxes.

SCORE 1 3

Brain Quest Math Workbook: Pre-Kindergarten

Train Time

Color the shapes to make a train.

Robots

Trace the shapes to draw a robot.
Then use shapes to draw your own robot.

Buttons

A pattern is something that repeats.
Look at the buttons.
The green and blue buttons make a pattern.

Color the next button in each pattern.

Maracas

Circle the next maraca in each pattern.

Pretty Patterns

Circle the next shape in each pattern.

The Right Size

Circle the next bird in each pattern.

Shapes and Patterns

Flower Power

Color the last flower in each pattern.

All Clean!

Color the last item of clothing in each pattern.

Cool School

Circle the next item in each pattern.

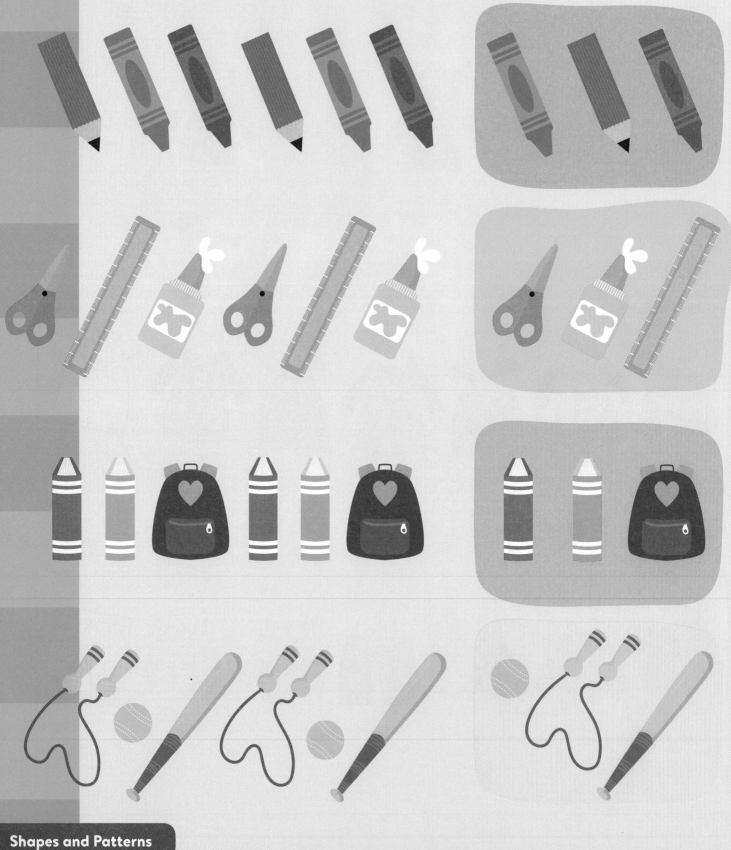

Night Sky

Circle the next group in each pattern.

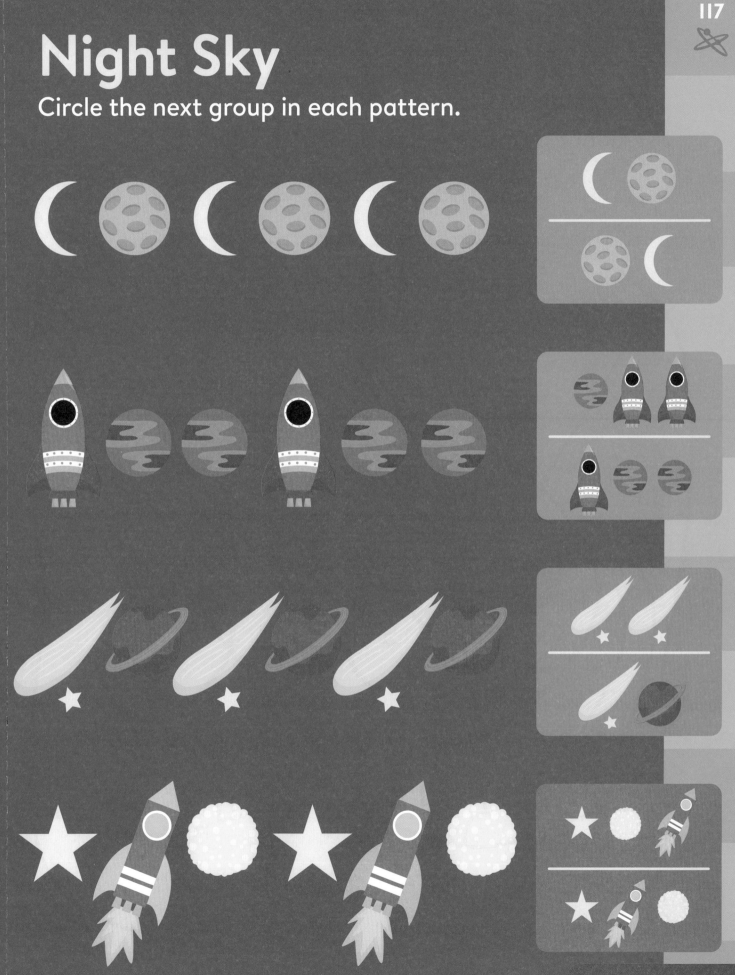

Shapes and Patterns

Fish Tales

Color by number.
What animal did you make?

1 2 3 4 5

Brain Quest Math Workbook: Pre-Kindergarten

Sweet as Honey

Color by number. See who is waving at you!

6 7 8 9 10

You are in great shape! Put a sticker on your map!

Line Up

Ordinal numbers tell place or position.
Circle the 1st kid in line.

first 1st   second 2nd   third 3rd   fourth 4th   fifth 5th

Circle the 2nd and 4th runners.

1st

Outer Space

Draw an X on the 1st and 2nd planets.

1st

Circle the 3rd and 5th astronauts.

1st

Color the 4th rocket **orange**.
Color the other rockets **red**.

1st

Order and Position

Ice Cold

Ordinal numbers can go in either direction!
Draw an X on the 1st and 3rd whales.

Draw an X on the 2nd and 5th seals.

Draw an X on the 3rd and 4th penguins.

Travel Time

Color the 1st car **blue** and the 5th car **green**.
Color the 2nd boat **pink**.
Color the 3rd boat **purple**.

1st place!
Nice job!

Order and Position

Bugs in a Row

1st

Draw a line from each insect to the number and word that show its place in line.

1st — first

2nd — second

3rd — third

4th — fourth

5th — fifth

Above and Below

The cat is **above** the table.
The yarn is **below** the table.

Circle each cat that is **above** the yarn.
Draw an X on each cat that is **below** the yarn.

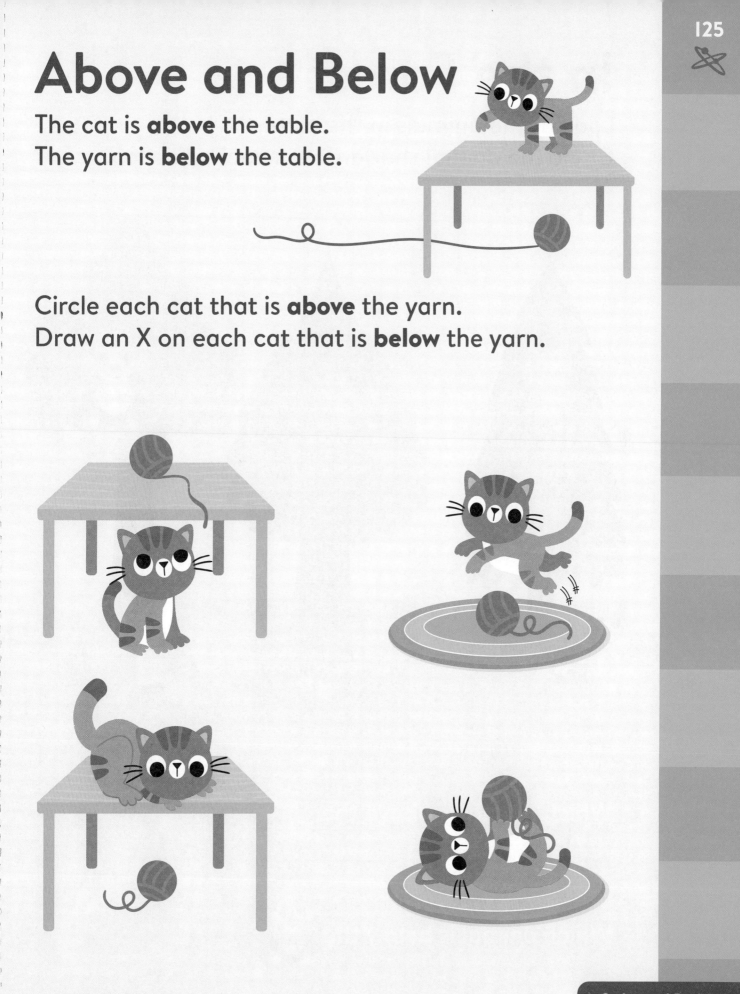

Order and Position

In the Forest

Look at the animals in the picture.
Circle the animal that answers each question.

Which animal is **above** the ?

Which animal is **below** the ?

Brain Quest Math Workbook: Pre-Kindergarten

Parade

The trumpeter is **in front of** the bike.
The wagon is **behind** the bike.

Color the picture that shows the drummer **in front of** the trumpeter.

Color the picture that shows the wagon **behind** the dog.

Order and Position

Fire Station

Read each sentence.
Circle **in front of** or **behind** .

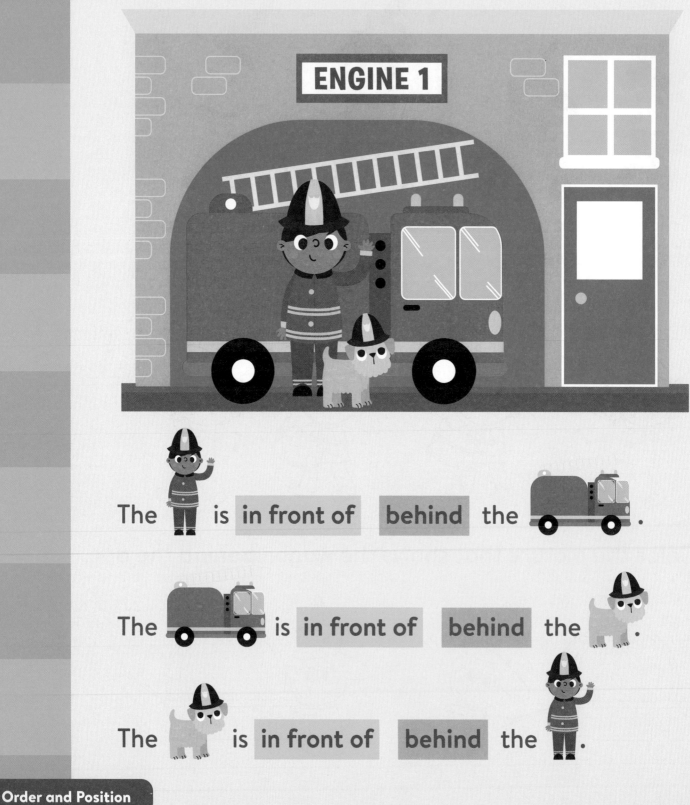

The 🧑‍🚒 is **in front of** **behind** the 🚒 .

The 🚒 is **in front of** **behind** the 🐕 .

The 🐕 is **in front of** **behind** the 🧑‍🚒 .

The Play House

Amanda is **inside** the house.
The dog and the cat are **outside** the house.

Color the toys **inside** the toy box **brown**.
Color the toys **outside** the toy box **blue**.

Order and Position

Yum! Yum!

Draw an apple **inside** Amanda's lunch box.

Draw a banana **outside** Amanda's lunch box.

In the Park

Draw a sun **above** the merry-go-round.
Draw a flower **in front of** the tree.
Draw a sandcastle **inside** the sandbox.

Order and Position

Alligators

Draw a line between each alligator and the word that tells where the alligator is.

above

below

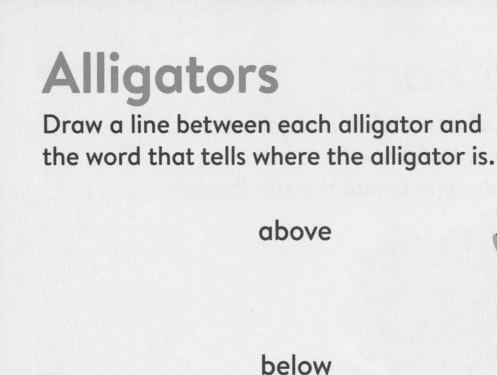

in front of

behind

Great job!
Put a sticker
on your map!

inside

outside

Measure This!

Color the **longer** fence **green**.
Color the **shorter** fence **pink**.

longer   **shorter**

Color the **taller** haystack **green**.
Color the **shorter** haystack **pink**.

Color the **heavier** pig **green**.
Color the **lighter** pig **pink**.

lighter

heavier

taller   **shorter**

You can compare things in different ways!

Measurement

Longer, Shorter

Circle the **longer** rope in each group.
Draw an X on the **shorter** rope in
each group.

Brain Quest Math Workbook: Pre-Kindergarten

Taller, Shorter

Circle the **taller** object in each group.
Draw an X on the **shorter** object in each group.

Measurement

Taller, Shorter

Look at the tree.
Draw a **shorter** tree.

Look at the bird house.
Draw a **taller** bird house.

Heavier, Lighter

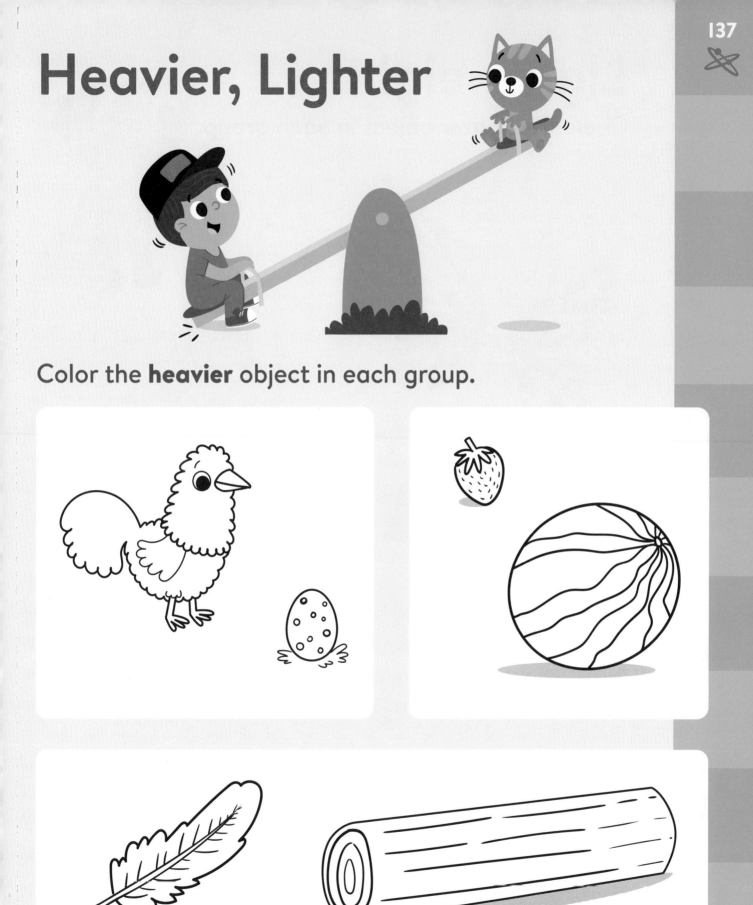

Color the **heavier** object in each group.

Measurement

Lightweight

Circle the **lighter** object in each group.

Dino Fun!

Color the **taller** dinosaur in each group.

Measurement

Who's the Longest?

Circle the **longer** toy animal in each group.

Up and Down

Draw something that is **heavier** than a mouse.

Draw something that is **lighter** than an elephant.

Measurement

More Than a Cat

Color each animal that is **heavier** than a cat.

Brain Quest Math Workbook: Pre-Kindergarten

Window Shopping

What numbers do you see?

BAKERY

MARKET

8

10

Count the items in the shops.
Write the number of each item in the box.

There are ⬚ 🥧.
pies

There are ⬚ 🫙.
jars

There are ⬚ 🧁.
cupcakes

There are ⬚ 🥫.
cans

Measurement

I Spy!

Count the objects you see.
Write the number of each object in the box.

	people		trees		dogs
	fountain		squirrels		birds

All About Me

How old are you?
Color I cupcake for every year.

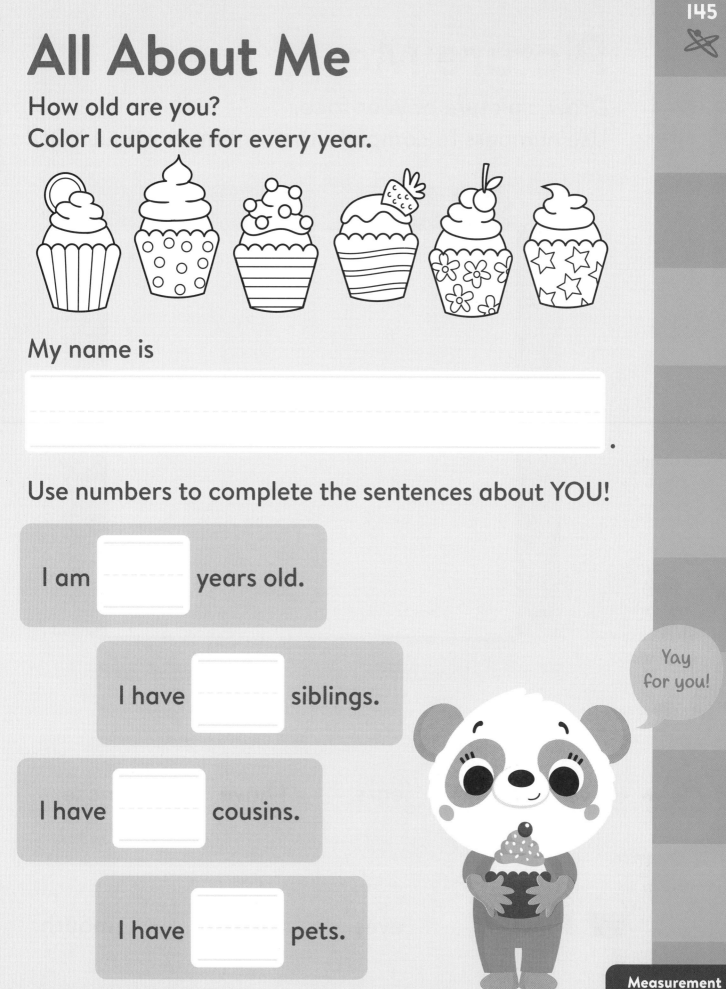

My name is

_____

Use numbers to complete the sentences about YOU!

I am [ ] years old.

I have [ ] siblings.

I have [ ] cousins.

I have [ ] pets.

Yay for you!

Measurement

Picture Me

Draw a picture of your face.
Use numbers to complete the sentences about YOU!

Great job! Put a sticker on your map!

I have ☐ ears.

I have ☐ nose.

I have ☐ eyes.

I have ☐ mouth.

Measurement

Glossary

first
1st

second
2nd

third
3rd

fourth
4th

fifth
5th

Brain Quest Math Workbook: Pre-Kindergarten

0 zero

1 one

2 two

3 three

4 four

5 five

6 six

7 seven

8 eight

9 nine

10 ten

Brain Quest Math Workbook: Pre-Kindergarten

rectangle

square

circle

triangle

same

different

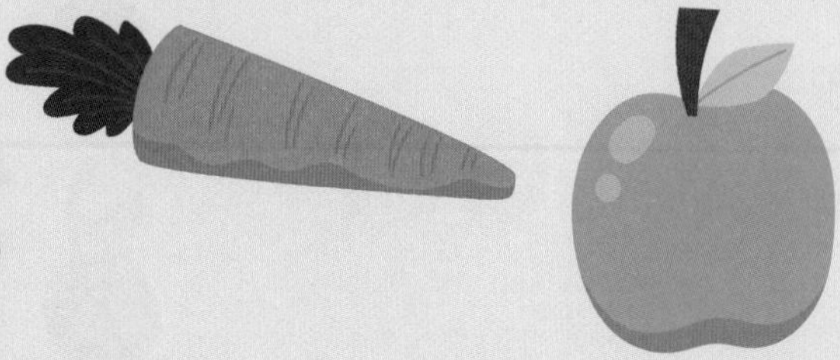

QUESTIONS

Which kid has 3 balloons?

BRAIN QUEST®

QUESTIONS

Which player has more balls?

BRAIN QUEST®

QUESTIONS

Which animals belong in a group?

BRAIN QUEST®

QUESTIONS

Which 3 are the same shape?

BRAIN QUEST®

QUESTIONS

How many red stripes are on this flag?

BRAIN QUEST®

QUESTIONS

How many eggs are in the nest?

BRAIN QUEST®

Brain Quest Mini-Deck

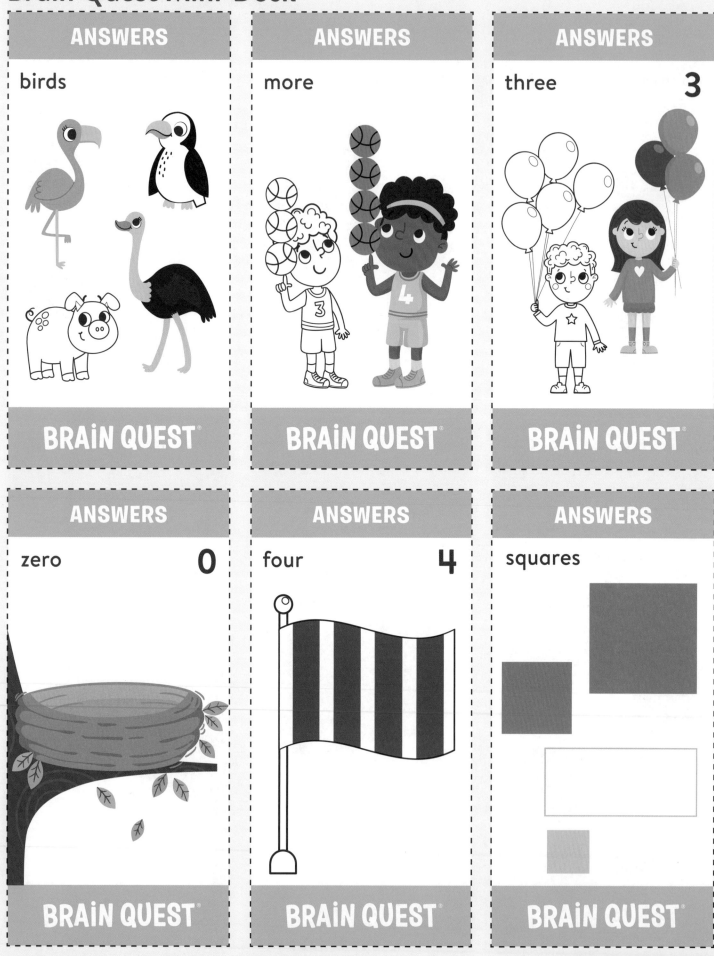

ANSWERS

birds

BRAIN QUEST

ANSWERS

more

BRAIN QUEST

ANSWERS

three 3

BRAIN QUEST

ANSWERS

zero 0

BRAIN QUEST

ANSWERS

four 4

BRAIN QUEST

ANSWERS

squares

BRAIN QUEST

Brain Quest Mini-Deck

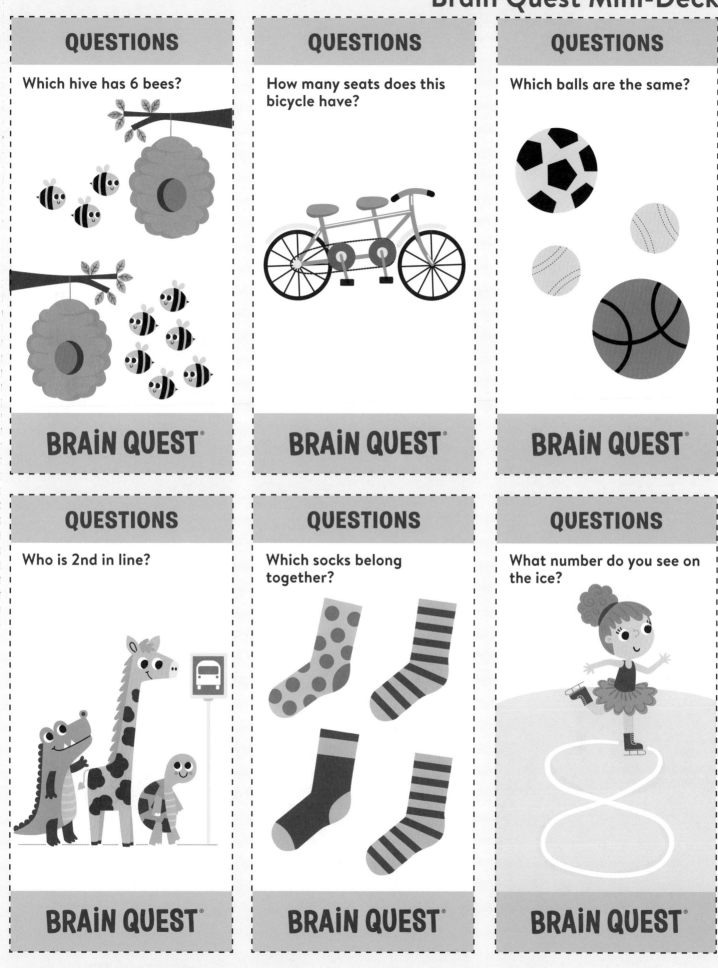

QUESTIONS

Which hive has 6 bees?

BRAIN QUEST

QUESTIONS

How many seats does this bicycle have?

BRAIN QUEST

QUESTIONS

Which balls are the same?

BRAIN QUEST

QUESTIONS

Who is 2nd in line?

BRAIN QUEST

QUESTIONS

Which socks belong together?

BRAIN QUEST

QUESTIONS

What number do you see on the ice?

BRAIN QUEST

Brain Quest Math Workbook: Pre-Kindergarten

Brain Quest Mini-Deck

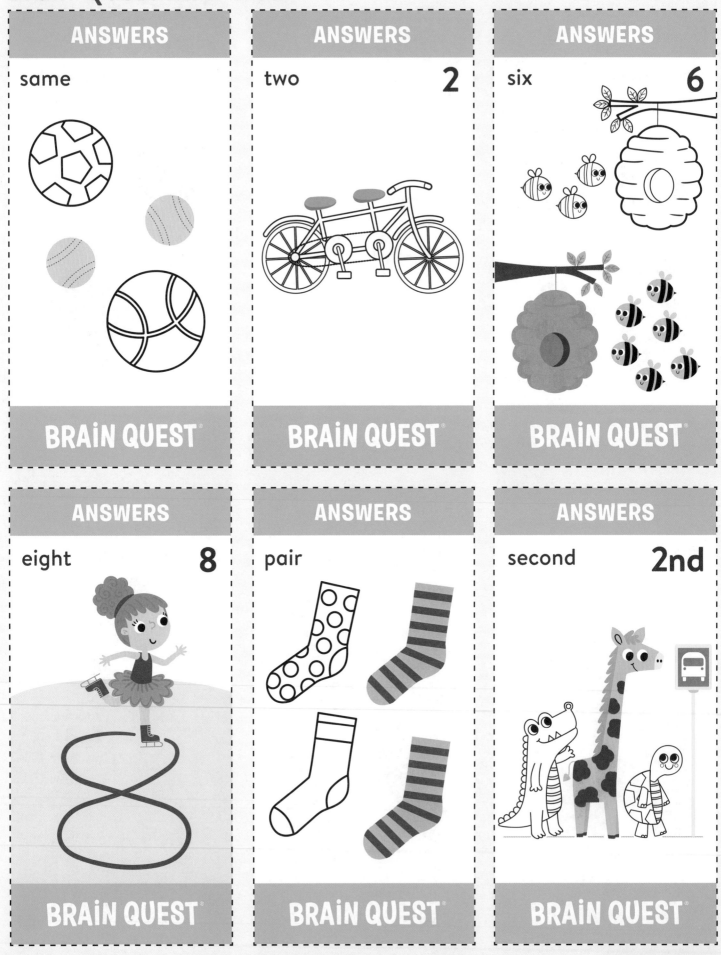

ANSWERS

same

BRAIN QUEST®

ANSWERS

two   **2**

BRAIN QUEST®

ANSWERS

six   **6**

BRAIN QUEST®

ANSWERS

eight   **8**

BRAIN QUEST®

ANSWERS

pair

BRAIN QUEST®

ANSWERS

second   **2nd**

BRAIN QUEST®

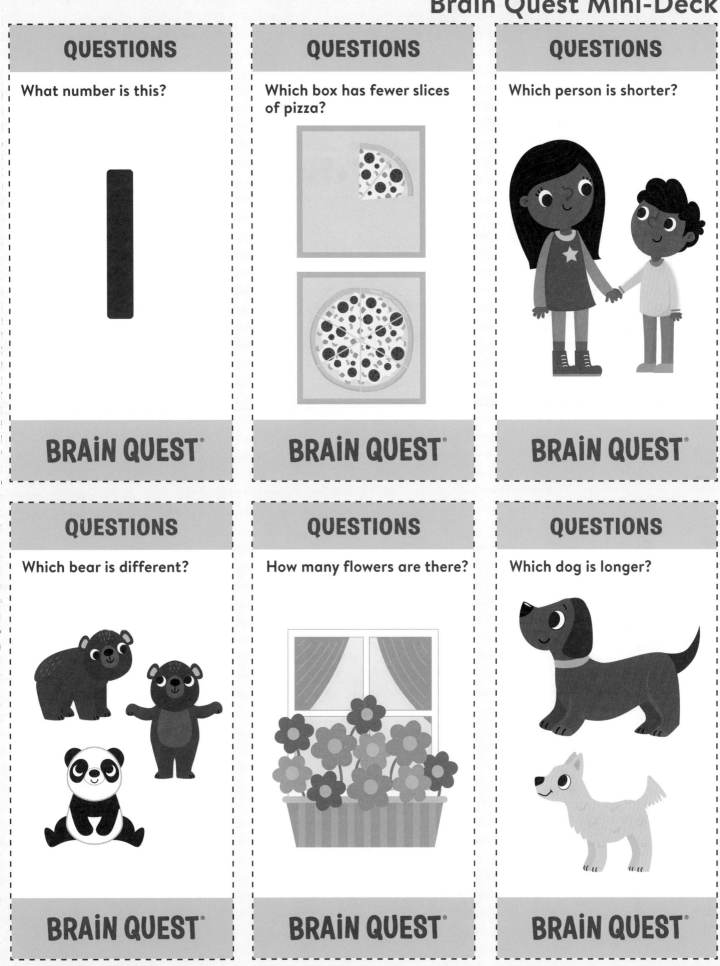

QUESTIONS

What number is this?

BRAIN QUEST

QUESTIONS

Which box has fewer slices of pizza?

BRAIN QUEST

QUESTIONS

Which person is shorter?

BRAIN QUEST

QUESTIONS

Which bear is different?

BRAIN QUEST

QUESTIONS

How many flowers are there?

BRAIN QUEST

QUESTIONS

Which dog is longer?

BRAIN QUEST

Brain Quest Mini-Deck

ANSWERS

shorter

BRAIN QUEST

ANSWERS

fewer

BRAIN QUEST

ANSWERS

one   1

BRAIN QUEST

ANSWERS

longer

BRAIN QUEST

ANSWERS

ten   10

BRAIN QUEST

ANSWERS

different

BRAIN QUEST

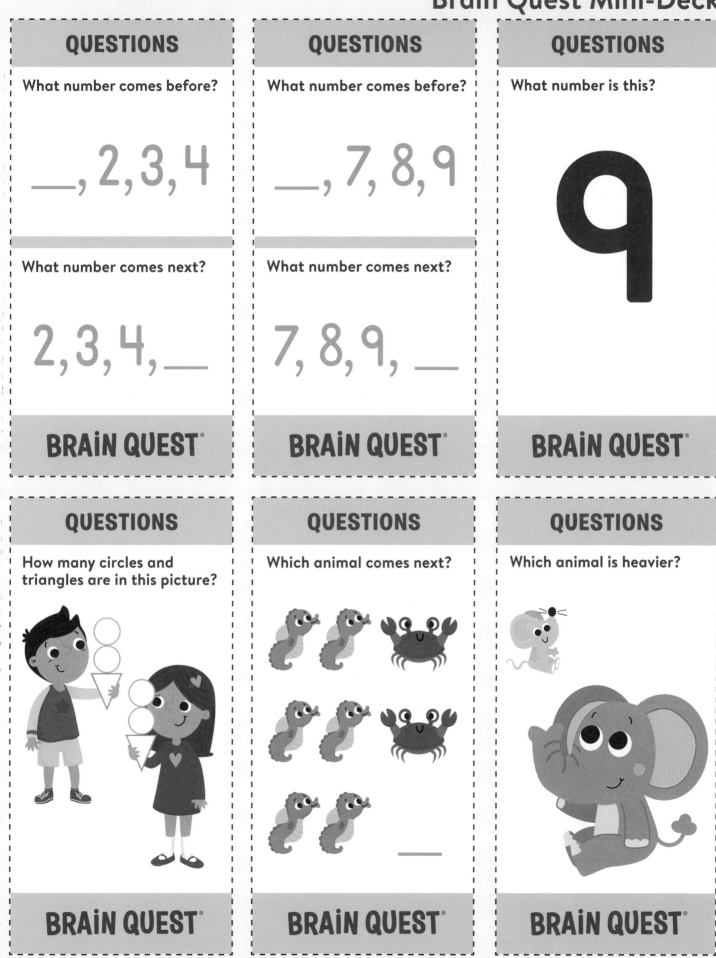

QUESTIONS

What number comes before?

__, 2, 3, 4

What number comes next?

2, 3, 4, __

BRAIN QUEST®

QUESTIONS

What number comes before?

__, 7, 8, 9

What number comes next?

7, 8, 9, __

BRAIN QUEST®

QUESTIONS

What number is this?

9

BRAIN QUEST®

QUESTIONS

How many circles and triangles are in this picture?

BRAIN QUEST®

QUESTIONS

Which animal comes next?

__

BRAIN QUEST®

QUESTIONS

Which animal is heavier?

BRAIN QUEST®

Brain Quest Math Workbook: Pre-Kindergarten

Brain Quest Mini-Deck

ANSWERS

nine **9**

ANSWERS

six **6**

6, 7, 8, 9

ten **10**

7, 8, 9, **10**

ANSWERS

one **1**

1, 2, 3, 4

five **5**

2, 3, 4, **5**

BRAIN QUEST®

BRAIN QUEST®

BRAIN QUEST®

ANSWERS

heavier

ANSWERS

a crab

ANSWERS

4 circles

2 triangles

BRAIN QUEST®

BRAIN QUEST®

BRAIN QUEST®

CERTIFICATE OF ACHIEVEMENT

Earned by

for completing all sections in the

BRAIN QUEST®

PRE-KINDERGARTEN MATH WORKBOOK